Spy Skills for Girls

with Devon Danby

By Carmen Wright

Illustrated by Ilaria Campana

Bright Green Books

Bright Green Books

Spy Skills for Girls
Published by Bright Green Books
www.brightgreenbooks.com

Copyright © 2011 Carmen Wright

First Print Edition: December 2014
Second Print Edition: August 2021

First eBook Edition: December 2011
Second eBook Edition: August 2021

Text by Carmen Wright
Cover and illustrations by Ilaria Campana
Book design by Carmen Wright

ISBN: 978-0-9881256-3-6 (Paperback)
ISBN: 978-0-9881256-4-3 (Hardcover)
ISBN: 978-0-9881256-2-9 (eBook)

Table of Contents

A message from Devon

Sooner or later, every girl needs to do a little spying.

Why is your sister acting strangely?

What is that sneaky boy hiding in his backpack?

To find out, you need skills. Spy skills.

And I'm just the girl to teach you.

I'm Devon Danby and I'm a spy. Well, actually, I'm not REALLY Devon Danby. That's a fake name. But the spy part is true.

My spy training started in third grade. I went to special spy classes every day after school and on weekends. Imagine all the fun times I missed out on!

Luckily, you don't have to worry about any of that. I've packed all my BEST spy skills into this one little book.

Once you've learned these basic skills, be sure to share them with your best Spygirl friends!

Here's my #1 tip: always be sure to keep yourself and your Spygirl friends safe.
If something or someone seems really dangerous or scary, be sure to talk to an adult. That's what I do.

Now, on to your training...

Devon

Why Spy?

The truth is, most people spy everyday.

Do you notice where your dad hides his favourite cookies? Do you know what time your mom takes her shower? Do you know which way your friend walks home from school?

That's like spying. Only spying is much more than that.

When you spy, you make a plan to find out information.

Who to watch. When to watch. What's important and what's not.

Sometimes, you can spy on your own. But most of the time, it's easier to have another Spygirl help you out.

And more fun, too!

Spy words

Let's start by going over some important spy words.

Spy

A spy uncovers information about suspicious people and what they are doing.

Spygirl

You are a Spygirl! Ask your friends if they want to be Spygirls, too.

Spy Kit

An easy-to-carry container that contains small but important spy gear.

Spy Bag

A larger bag to hold your Spy Kit and other supplies, like disguises.

Suspect

Any suspicious person could be your suspect.

Decoy

A decoy is a fake message or person. It could be used by a suspect to confuse you. Or, you could use a decoy to confuse your suspect!

Drop

When you leave a message or an object for another Spygirl, the place you leave it is called a drop.

Shadowing

Following your suspect without them noticing is called shadowing.

Tail

A tail is someone who is shadowing you, or another person.

Spy supplies

A Spygirl needs to have her spy supplies ready at all times. For everyday spying, you only need a small Spy Kit. It can be hidden in your purse or backpack.

For bigger jobs, especially with disguises, you'll need a Spy Bag.

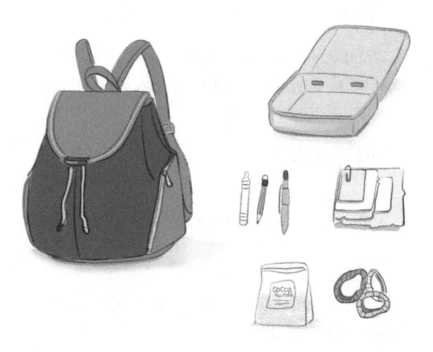

Spy Kit

A Spy Kit can be an empty candy tin or other small container with a lid that stays closed.

You'll need to fit in:

- White wax crayon

- Cocoa powder to read invisible ink

- White paper, cut or folded into small pieces

- Short wooden pencil

- Mini gel pen

- Elastics for your hair

Spy Bag

A Spy Bag needs to hold more supplies. Pick the best one for your mission and tuck in:

- Your smaller Spy Kit

- Disguise supplies: hat, sweater, sunglasses

- Folding travel mirror

- Lip gloss

- Baby powder and a small make-up brush to check for fingerprints

- Wide clear tape (not magic tape)

- Shiny black paper

- Magnifying glass

- Measuring tape

- Flashlight

- Thin cotton gloves, white or black

- String, scissors and large paper clips, to fish things out of a tight spot

- Water and snacks, when you will be out on a long mission (bring quiet snacks – not chips in noisy packages!)

- Plastic snack bags that can zip closed, for storing evidence

- Camera (or camera phone)

- Watch (or clock on your phone)

SPY TIP: Powders can be tricky to carry and messy to use. Measure out one tablespoon of each powder and store it in a small container with a secure lid. Round, plastic pill containers work well and snap closed. Or, use a mini jam jar.

Powers of Observation

Every good spy needs to keep their eyes open and remember what they see. Even a small detail can be very important.

Take notice of what people wear, how they walk and who they talk to. Watch to see if they are passing objects or messages to anyone.

Most people follow patterns of movement. Where does the suspect go and at what time? When do they eat dinner?

Keep notes and soon you'll know where to find your suspect without having to follow them around all day.

SPY TIP: Want to confuse an enemy spy? Change your patterns. If you usually walk the dog before you eat breakfast, switch it around. Eat breakfast first and then walk the dog.

Shadowing

Following your suspect can be tricky. If you act strangely, they will become suspicious. Here are some tricks to blend in.

Mix it up

Use your quick change supplies to slip on a disguise. Or, take turns and let another Spygirl shadow the suspect for a while.

Check your mirror

Pretend you're not watching at all. Turn your back on your suspect. Pull out a small mirror and put on some lip gloss. Then, watch them using your mirror.

Use your eyes

Watch your suspect with your eyes, not with your whole body. Don't move your head or shoulders. Just shift your eyes from side to side. This is easier with sunglasses on.

Stops and starts

Don't copy your suspect's moves. If they stop, keep moving until you have a good reason to stop. If they start moving, wait before you follow. Keep your distance.

Hide in a crowd

Use the people around you to cover your movements. Walk next to a family to blend in with them. Hide behind a grown-up to move across an open area. If someone is making a commotion, use the distraction to get closer to your suspect.

The quick change

Sometimes a spy must change how they look – and fast! Luckily, this is easy for girls. Just put a few extra things in your Spy Bag, and you'll be ready.

A hat or two

Hats are always a good idea. Try a baseball cap or a hat with a wide brim. Both can be pulled down low to hide your face.

Elastic hair bands

If you have long hair, you can use elastic hair bands to quickly change your hairstyle. Slip them into your pocket or tuck them into your Spy Kit.

Spy tip: Practice putting your hair up into a high ponytail and twist it to make an easy bun. Stick on a baseball cap and your hair has disappeared!

Sunglasses

Every spy needs a good pair of dark sunglasses. People will have a hard time remembering your face if they can't see your eyes. And no one will be able to see who or what you're looking at.

Jacket or sweater

Was that girl wearing blue or red? Confuse people by changing your clothes. Change your outfit by taking off your sweater, or by throwing on a big jacket to disguise what you're wearing. Expert spies turn their coats inside out for a whole new look.

Even change your Spy Bag!

Tuck a large, shopping tote into your Spy Bag. Once you're done your quick change, put your Spy Bag inside your tote. Shopping anyone?

Body doubles

Here's a cool trick. If you think you are being tailed, try using a body double. A body double looks like you and leads the enemy away while you do a quick change and escape. Follow these easy steps:

1. Ask another Spygirl to dress exactly like you.

2. Your Spygirl friend waits at a planned meeting place where she can hide. It could be behind a store display or a large sign or in a changing room.

3. When you are being tailed, take your time before you get to the meeting place. As soon as you are hidden from view, stop.

4. Give your hat, tote or sunglasses to your Spygirl friend so she looks even more like you.

5. Your Spygirl friend will step into view, keep walking, and pretend to be you.

6. You do a quick change and after a few minutes, go off in another direction.

7. Once you're safely away, the other Spygirl shows who she really is! She needs to act like she wasn't pretending to be you in the first place. Usually, taking off the hat will do the trick.

The enemy spy will see they made a mistake, but won't know where you went!

DISGUISES

What if you want to want to observe a suspect, but can't shadow them because you're going to be stuck in one place, like a library or at the park?

You don't want them to recognize you, but there's no place to hide.

In these cases, it's best to be in disguise. Dress differently than usual and use a Spy Bag that matches. Take on a new attitude. Change the way you move your body.

With a great disguise, the suspect will notice something unusual and may even look right at you.

But they will be so distracted by your attitude, your clothes and your props, they won't even notice that it's you!

Here are some of my favourite disguises.

Girly girl

Clothes: Dresses, skirts and tops with frills or sparkles. Shiny or furry jackets. A pretty purse. Fancy shoes. Dangly earrings.

Hair and make-up: Styled hair. Hair clips or hair bands. Pink lip gloss.

Attitude: Stand tall with your chin up. Avoid mud puddles and sports fields. Talk about fashion, famous singers or your dance class.

Skater girl

Clothes: Jeans or long shorts. Trendy tee-shirt or tank top. Lots of layers under a baggy sweater or hoodie. Flat skater-style runners. If you skate, bring along your board.

Hair and make-up: Relaxed hairstyle. Try a cool hat, like a knitted beanie or a baseball cap with a skater brand name. No make-up.

Attitude: Slouch over when you walk. Lean against walls or railings. Don't be in a big hurry. Talk about skate tricks, biking or when you plan to go surfing.

DRAMA GIRL

Clothes: Funky skirts or pants. Tops and jackets with fringes, bling, or spikes. Crazy mix of styles and colors. Flat black shoes or chunky boots. Unusual earrings. Lots of necklaces and bracelets.

Hair and make-up: Unique hair in wild styles with colored hair pieces clipped in. Bright eye shadow and lip gloss.

Attitude: Don't be afraid to attract attention. Use lots of arm motions and plenty of emotion. Talk about serious actors, drama class or your last big audition.

BOSS GIRL

Clothes: Cool jacket with pants or a skirt – they don't need to match. White top with buttons and a collar. Boots or shoes with a low heel. A watch. Large black tote bag with long handles.

Hair and make-up: Styled hair. Simple make-up and red lip gloss. Glasses or sunglasses.

Attitude: Serious and smart. Walk with confidence. Talk as if you run the place. Take control and tell people what to do.

Stealth girl

This disguise is used for times when you don't want to be seen.

Clothes: Fitted black pants and top. Quiet black shoes. Slim spy belt around your waist. Cover everything with a dark jacket.

Hair and make-up: Smooth your hair back into a ponytail or wear a black baseball cap. No lip gloss, but dark eyeliner would be cool.

Attitude: Quick, sly movements. Tuck into corners, behind lockers or inside doorways. Don't talk at all.

Your disguise ideas

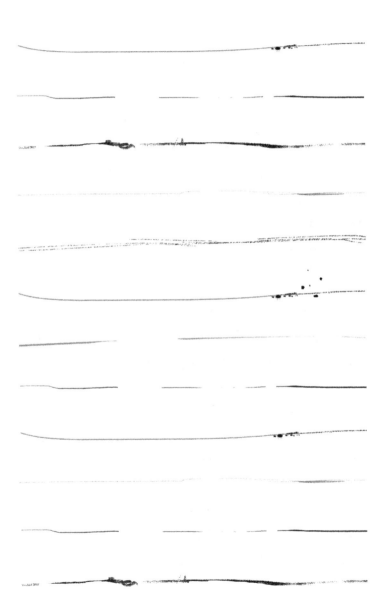

How to search a room

Your suspect is away and you need to find out what they're hiding, and fast!

Watch for traps

Before you go in the room or open anything, check for any traps. Watch for tape stuck across the door frame or desk drawers. Once the tape breaks, the suspect will know you've been there.

Smart searching

Take a good look around the room. Is there anything unusual or out of place?

Check the desk or dresser. Hunt for anything hidden on the bookshelves. Look inside small containers and drawers.

Be sure to search underneath clothes or behind books. Don't forget to look under the bed and under the mattress.

Anything hidden?

Check for secret hiding places. Is one shelf not as deep as the others? Is the storage box too shallow on the inside? Does the closet seem extra narrow?

Maybe there's a space hidden. Tap the wall or box to see if it sounds hollow and look for a way to open it.

SPY TIP: It's very important to make sure your search stays a secret. Put everything back exactly as you found it. And never read anyone's diary or journal. That's private!

Fingerprints

What if you think your suspect has been searching your room?

First, look to see whether anything has been disturbed. Then, check any disturbed spots for fingerprints.

Fingerprints are different for everybody. Match a mysterious fingerprint with a person, and you've got your suspect.

FINDING AND COLLECTING A PRINT

1. First look for sticky fingerprints on hard surfaces like glass, mirrors, desks or counters.

2. Softly brush the prints with enough powder to show the print clearly.

3. If you can't see a print, try dusting where you *think* a print might be.

4. Gently blow away any extra powder.

5. Press a piece of tape over the dusted print. Peel it away carefully.

6. Stick the tape on a piece of shiny black paper.

Need to take a fingerprint?

1. Using the side of a regular pencil, rub a wide, dark mark on a piece of paper.

2. Rub the finger on the black mark. Be sure it is covered with the dark dust.

3. Press a piece of tape firmly onto the finger.

4. Gently peel off the tape.

5. Stick the tape to a white piece of paper.

6. Use a magnifying glass to compare the found print with the ones you've taken. Look for similar patterns.

Shoe prints

If you are searching outside and the dirt is soft and damp, you could find a shoe print from your suspect.

Measure the shoe size using a measuring tape. Find out the shoe style. Did the shoe have high heels? Was it a flat flip-flop?

Check out the grip patterns on the bottom of runners to figure out the brand of shoe.

Draw or take a picture to help you remember.

Get-away plans

What if you're caught or someone spots you spying? This is no time for a chat. It's time to disappear.

Before you start a search, make a get-away plan. Where is the nearest door? Is there another way out? Is there a place to hide if you can't get out?

When you are shadowing a suspect, keep an eye open for places to hide or disappear. This can be as easy as slipping into a shop in the mall or ducking behind a tree.

Spy Tip: Plan ahead. Make up a good excuse to explain why you're there, just in case you're questioned.

Secret codes

Spygirls need to share the latest information on their suspects. Codes hide your messages from enemy spies. Important messages should always be sent in code.

The easiest codes are substitution codes, where one letter replaces another.

13-LETTER SWAP

Write down the first thirteen letters of the alphabet in a row. Underneath, match up the next thirteen letters.

```
A  B  C  D  E  F  G  H  I  J  K  L  M
N  O  P  Q  R  S  T  U  V  W  X  Y  Z
```

When you want to write the message, for a letter in the top row like the letter M, use the letter right underneath, which is the letter Z. For a letter on the bottom row like the letter T, use the letter just above, which is the letter G.

```
M E E T   M E   A T   T W O
```
becomes
```
Z R R G   Z R   N G   G J B
```

Key word swap

Use a key word to shift the alphabet over. Pick a word, like STAR, where no letter is used more than once.

Start your substitution with your key word. Then, use the rest of the alphabet. Skip over the letters you already used in your keyword.

A	B	C	D	E	F	G	H	I	J	K	L	M
S	T	A	R	B	C	D	E	F	G	H	I	J

N	O	P	Q	R	S	T	U	V	W	X	Y	Z
K	L	M	N	O	P	Q	U	V	W	X	Y	Z

M E E T M E A T T W O
becomes
J H H Q J H S Q Q W L

Try writing this message in code using the same STAR key word swap:

BE CAREFUL THE

SUSPECT IS NEAR THE

DROP SPOT

SPY TIP: Be sure to change the key word often.

Answer on the page 64...

Magazine code

Find a page in a magazine with lots of words. Use a pin to prick a tiny hole under the words you need for your message.

Pass the magazine to anther Spygirl. Tell her to read the interesting story about rabbits.

To read the code, find the story and hold up that page to the light. Using a highlighter pen, mark the words above each tiny hole you find.

Then, put the magazine down, find all the highlighter marks and write down the words to find the hidden message.

Breaking a Code

Code breaking takes time. Use a pencil and have an eraser ready. Write out the coded message. Leave lots of space underneath it.

When you figure out one of the letters, write it every time you see that letter in your code.

Common words and patterns can help you break a code. Here are a few tips:

Single Letters

There are only two letters that stand on their own. A and I. Look for these first.

Double Letters

Not all letters like to hang out with their twin. Double vowels are EE or OO. Double consonants are DD, PP, LL, SS, MM and NN.

Common letters, common words

Try matching the most common letters, E, H, S and T. Keep an eye out for the word THE, the most used three-letter word.

Vowels are needed

Each word must have at least one vowel. Check for patterns where A, E, I, O, U and even Y may fit.

Test your skills!

Try to break these coded messages.

Hint: try a 13-letter swap

O E V A T   L B H E

F C L X V G   G B   F P U B B Y

Z B A Q N L

Answer on the page 64...

Hint: you found this coded message when you were at the shop buying FLOWERS for your mom.

B   V B G G   H E E Q   Y J T

F Q   Q A E   H F G G   F Q

Q V J

Answer on the page 64...

Invisible ink

Writing in invisible ink can help keep your message a secret.

1. If you have a white wax crayon, you can use that.

2. If not, you need soft wax from a white candle. Have a grown-up break off a piece of wax from a white candle that's been warmed up a bit. Take the wax and roll it between your hands. Shape it into a crayon.

3. Take your white wax crayon and write your message on white paper.

4. Write a decoy message in pen on top of your invisible message.

Reading invisible ink

To see the invisible ink, take a pinch of cocoa powder and sprinkle it on the paper.

Using your finger, lightly rub the cocoa across the page.

The powder won't stick to the wax and the message becomes visible!

SPY TIP: Be smart. Even though your ink is invisible, make sure your message is in code.

Swaps and drops

Now your message is written in code or even in invisible ink. How do you get it to another Spygirl without being seen?

Try using a drop or a swap.

The message swap

Get two bags that look exactly the same. Keep one. The second bag goes to the other Spygirl. Arrange a time and place to do the swap.

Put the secret message in your bag. At the meeting place, put your bags down while you say hello.

Then, pick up the other bag when you go. Your bag with the secret message goes with the other Spygirl.

No one will know you made the swap!

SPY TIP: This swap also works if you need to swap spy stuff, like a hat for a disguise or a magnifying glass and fingerprint samples.

THE DROP

A drop is when you leave the item and walk away. Agree on a drop spot with another Spygirl. The spot needs to be easy to find, but not obvious to others.

Disguise your message and hide it in the drop spot. Later on, the other Spygirl will go to the spot and pick up your message.

MESSAGE DISGUISES

- Wrap your message around a stick and cover with brown string.

- Tape your message on the back of a big leaf.

- Tape your message under a rock.

- Tuck your message inside a note book.

- Leave your message inside a paper shopping bag.

Cool drop spots

- Under the slide

- Behind a picture

- In a rock garden

- Inside a book in the library

- Under a chair or bench

SPY TIP: Be aware when using some drop locations, like in a mall. Your Spygirl friend better be there fast – otherwise mall security could find your message and throw it away!

Signs and countersigns

If you can *see* another Spygirl but can't *talk* to her, you can still send a message.

Plan ahead for this and work out a secret code using body language.

Expert spies use everyday moves in a special combination to pass along messages.

Everyday moves

- Tuck your hair behind your right ear

- Scratch your forehead

- Rub your nose

- Tie your left shoe

- Sneeze, cough or laugh

- Put on lip gloss

- Read a magazine

- Pull on your ear or earring

- Twirl your necklace

- Check out your fingernails

MESSAGE MOVES

Now, try these moves in a special order to send a message.

- Sneeze, rub your nose and pull on your earring means that the teacher is coming back to the classroom.

- Tie your shoe, check out your fingernails and tuck your hair behind your ear means that the suspect has left the playground.

- If you understand the message, let the other Spygirl know by twirling your necklace.

Other signs

Wear a special ring as a signal that you'll meet outside the music room after school.

Put your sweater on the back of your chair to let another Spygirl know there's a message waiting at the drop spot.

Final tips

Congratulations! You now have the skills you need to start spying.

Design your own disguises. Make your own secret codes. Share these spy skills with your best friends.

And remember, if you ever discover something that makes you uncomfortable or nervous, be sure to tell an adult.

Have fun and stay safe!

Devon

More practice with codes

Could you break the code?

Did you break the code on Page 45?

Use a key word swap with FLOWERS as the key word.

A	B	C	D	E	F	G	H	I	J	K	L	M
F	L	O	W	E	R	S	A	B	C	D	G	H

N	O	P	Q	R	S	T	U	V	W	X	Y	Z
I	J	K	M	N	P	Q	T	U	V	X	Y	Z

Here is that message again:

B   V B G G   H E E Q   Y J T

F Q   Q A E   H F G G   F Q

Q V J

Answer on the page 64...

Practice #1

Code this message using the 13-letter swap.

C H E C K   T H E   D O G ' S

C O L L A R   F O R   T H E

M E S S A G E

13-letter swap key:

A	B	C	D	E	F	G	H	I	J	K	L	M
N	O	P	Q	R	S	T	U	V	W	X	Y	Z

Answer on the page 64...

Practice #2

Decode this message using the 13-letter swap.

S V A Q   G U R   Z V F F V A T

N E G   C E B W R P G

O R U V A Q   G U R   T V N A G

J N Y Y   Z N C

13-letter swap key:

A B C D E F G H I J K L M
N O P Q R S T U V W X Y Z

Answer on the page 65...

Practice #3

Code your own message using the 13-letter swap.

_____   ___   ____

_____

_____   _____   _____

_____

_____   _____

_____   _____

13-letter swap key:

```
A  B  C  D  E  F  G  H  I  J  K  L  M
N  O  P  Q  R  S  T  U  V  W  X  Y  Z
```

Practice #4

Code this message using the key word swap where CAT is the key word.

D O   N O T   S T A Y   I N

T H E   C L A S S R O O M

D U R I N G   L U N C H

Create your code key using CAT:

A B C D E F G H I J K L M
C A T

N O P Q R S T U V W X Y Z

Answer on the page 65..

PRACTICE #5

Uncode this message using the CAT key word swap code.

W D   W H K K   M D D B   C

B H R F U H R D   W G D M

W D   E N K K N W   S G D

R U R O D T S   C S   S G D

O C Q J

Answer on the page 65...

Answers

From page 41:

T B   A S O B C U I   Q E B

P U P M B A Q   F P   K B S O

Q E B   R O L M   P M L Q

From page 44:

B R I N G   Y O U R

S P Y K I T   T O   S C H O O L

M O N D A Y

From pages 45 and 58:

I   W I L L   M E E T   Y O U

A T   T H E   M A L L   A T

T W O

From page 59:

P U R P X   G U R   Q B T ' F

P B Y Y N E   S B E   G U R

Z R F F N T R

From page 60:

F I N D   T H E   M I S S I N G
A R T   P R O J E C T
B E H I N D   T H E   G I A N T
W A L L   M A P

From page 62:

B N   M N S   R S C Y   H M
S G D   T K C R R Q N N L
B U Q H M F   K U M T G

From page 63:

W E   W I L L   N E E D   A
D I S G U I S E   W H E N
W E   F O L L O W   T H E
S U S P E C T   A T   T H E
P A R K

YOUR SPY NOTES

Your spy notes

Your spy notes

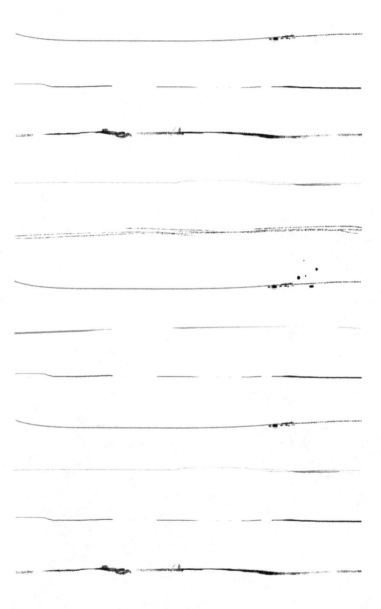

Want more?

Visit www.spyskillsforgirls.com

CARMEN WRIGHT is the author of Spy Skills for Girls and the Tri-City Mysteries. She has always loved mysteries and wishes she had better tips for spying and detecting back when she was a kid. Carmen lives in Coquitlam, British Columbia (Canada) with a golden labrador retriever, a golden cat and two inspiring daughters.

www.carmenwright.com

ILARIA CAMPANA is a character designer and illustrator living in a little town in the countryside of Rome (Italy). She loves animals and plants, having studied them for several years. When not drawing or building a time machine assisted by her cat, you can find her in the nearby mountains, observing wild animals.

ilariacampana.myportfolio.com
ilaria-campana.tumblr.com

CPSIA information can be obtained
at www.ICGtesting.com
Printed in the USA
LVHW081429021121
702246LV00002B/172

9 780988 125643

TEENAGE INDEX

Spending time with younger children is often easier than with teenagers, but it's more important than ever for parents to find a way to connect with their children between the ages of 13 and 18. Your child may enjoy any of the 700 activities listed in A Kid's Guide to Kansas City, but these listed below are specifically designed for teenagers and their parents. Good luck!

Also, check out the entire section on Family Voluntarism (pages 19-22). Not only does this provide some wonderful activities to do with your teenagers, it also looks good on college scholarship applications!

NOTES

_____

_____

_____

_____

_____

_____

_____

_____

_____

_____

_____

_____

_____

_____

_____

_____

_____